Little Pebble™

Transportation

Trucks

by Mari Schuh

CAPSTONE PRESS
a capstone imprint

Little Pebble is published by Capstone Press,
1710 Roe Crest Drive, North Mankato, Minnesota 56003
www.mycapstone.com

Library of Congress Cataloging-in-Publication Data
Library of Congress Cataloging-in-Publication data is available on the Library of Congress website.
ISBN: 978-1-5157-7300-9 (hardcover)
ISBN: 978-1-5157-7306-1 (paperback)
ISBN: 978-1-5157-7312-2 (eBook PDF)

Summary: Provides an overview of the features and the different types of trucks.

Editorial Credits
Carrie Braulick Sheely, editor; Lori Bye, designer; Wanda Winch, media researcher; Laura Manthe,
production specialist

Photo Credits
Alamy Stock Photo: Transport/Stephen Barnes, 8 – 9; Capstone Studio: Karon Dubke, 11; Dreamstime:
Davidebner, 21, Vitpho, cover, 5; iStockphoto: 8c061bbf_466, 12 – 13; Shutterstock: Kisan, Steel design,
Mario Pantelic, lines design, Mike Brake, 17, Robert J. Beyers II, 15, T. Sumaetho, zoom motion design,
TFoxFoto, 7, Tony Baggett, 19

Printed and bound in China.
010429F17

Table of Contents

On the Road

What's that noise?

A big truck goes down the road.

Here it comes!

Trucks haul loads.

They can carry dirt.

They can carry logs.

See them go!

Parts

Trucks have big engines.

They often use diesel fuel.

The cab is in the front.

The driver sits here.

She starts the engine.

Let's go!

Kinds

A tanker is long.

It can hold milk, oil, or gas.

A dump truck has a bed.

It holds heavy loads.

It tilts.

It dumps the load!

A fire truck puts out fires.

It has long hoses.

Whoosh!

They spray water.

A garbage truck is busy.

It picks up lots of trash.

It goes to the landfill.

Monster trucks have big wheels.

These trucks fly through the air.

They smash cars flat!

Glossary

bed—the back end of a dump truck; the bed tips up to dump loads

cab—an area for a driver to sit in a large truck or machine

diesel fuel—a heavy fuel that burns to make power

engine—a machine in which fuel burns to provide power

haul—to pull or carry a load

landfill—a place where garbage is buried

load—anything that must be lifted and carried by a vehicle, person, or machine

Read More

Adamson, Thomas K. *Garbage Trucks*. Mighty Machines in Action. Minneapolis: Bellwether Media, 2017.

Bach, Rachel. *The Monster Truck Race*. Let's Race. Mankato, Minn.: Amicus Ink, 2017.

Clay, Kathryn. *Dump Trucks*. Construction Vehicles at Work. North Mankato, Minn.: Capstone Press, 2017.

Internet Sites

Use FactHound to find Internet sites related to this book.

Visit *www.facthound.com*

Just type in 9781515773009 and go.

Check out projects, games and lots more at
www.capstonekids.com

Critical Thinking Questions

1. Name two parts that trucks often have in common.

2. Why might people use trucks instead of other vehicles?

3. Name two ways that trucks can help people.

Index